SEA SHELLS

THE SEA

Jason Cooper

The Rourke Corporation, Inc.
Vero Beach, Florida 32964

Edited by Sandra A. Robinson

PHOTO CREDITS
All photos © Lynn M. Stone except pages 7 and 10,
© Margarette Mead

LIBRARY OF CONGRESS
Library of Congress Cataloging-in-Publication Data
Cooper, Jason, 1942-
   Sea shells / by Jason Cooper.
   p.   cm. — (Discovery library of the sea)
   Includes index.
   Summary: Describes different kinds of mollusks, with information
on how their shells are formed, where they live, and how to collect
sea shells.
   ISBN 0-86593-233-6
   1. Shells—Juvenile literature. [1. Mollusks. 2. Shells.] I. Title.
II. Series: Cooper, Jason, 1942-   Discovery library of the sea.
QL405.2.C66   1992
594'.0471—dc20   92-16075
                                                CIP
                                                AC
Printed in the USA

TABLE OF CONTENTS

SEA SHELLS

Every empty sea shell was once the home of a soft, boneless little animal called a **mollusk.** The mollusk didn't borrow the shell as a place to live. It made the shell!

Certain kinds, or **species,** of mollusks make shells to protect their bodies. When the animal dies, its body is gobbled up by other **marine,** or sea, creatures. But the animal's hard shell remains—like a treasure waiting to be found.

Sea snail extending its foot and body from shell

TWO SHELLS, ONE ANIMAL

Mollusks such as clams are known as **bivalves** because they have two shells that clamp together. Bivalve shells are joined by a muscle hinge that opens and closes the two shell halves.

Most bivalves spend their adult lives attached to rocks or hidden in ocean sand and mud.

Many bivalves, including clams, oysters, mussels and scallops are important food for people.

Flame scallop is one of the most colorful bivalve mollusks

SINGLE SHELLS

One-shelled mollusks, such as conchs, are called snails. Snail shells may be quite fancy with twisting patterns and bright markings.

Snails withdraw into their shells like turtles. But by poking its head and body out, a snail can move slowly along rocks or the sea bottom.

The largest snail is the Florida horse conch. Its shell can be 24 inches long.

Florida horse conch, largest of the American marine snails

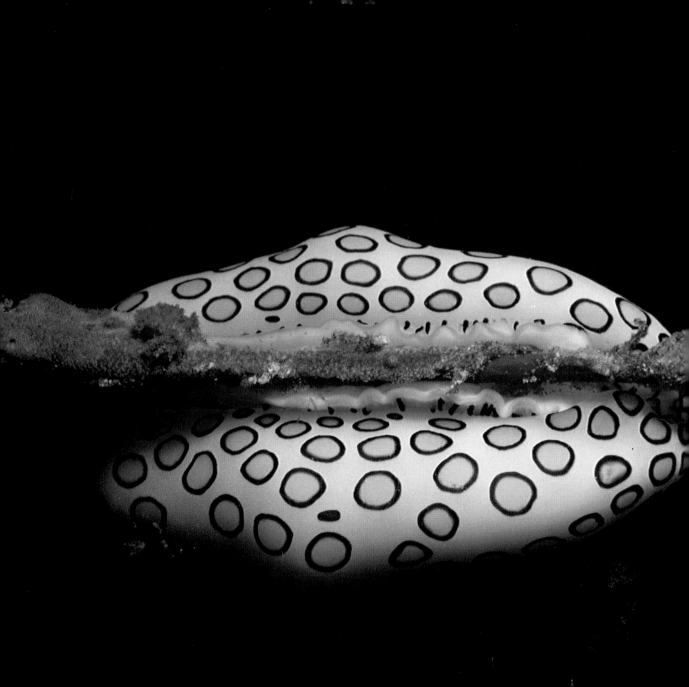

THE MAKING OF SEA SHELLS

One of a living sea shell's soft body parts is the **mantle.** The mantle works with other body parts to make liquids that harden into shell. As the animal inside the shell grows, it enlarges its shell.

Another body part, called the **foot,** makes a tough cover to seal up and protect the opening on the bottom of the shell. The cover is attached to the foot.

Adult mollusks lay tiny eggs. Some of them survive and grow into adults themselves.

Flamingo tongue snail wraps its spotted mantle around its shell

11

Junonia shell is both rare and beautiful

Inside view of an abalone shell, a favorite of jewelry makers

HOW SEA SHELLS LIVE

Most bivalve mollusks eat by straining, or filtering, tiny living things **(organisms)** from the water.

Many snails are grazers or **predators.** Grazers eat plant material in the sea. Predator snails eat other animals, including other snails. One of the fiercest shelled predators is the tulip snail.

The tulip snail is a predator of other snails

WHERE SEA SHELLS LIVE

Each species of marine mollusk needs certain things to live. Different kinds of mollusks live in different undersea **habitats,** or places, where their needs can be met.

Many conchs live in shallow water. But other mollusks may live in ocean water up to three miles deep!

The temperature of the ocean water and the kind of sea bottom also affect where the different kinds of mollusks can live.

Lettered olive snail lives on shallow, sandy shores

SHELLS ALONG THE BEACH

Almost all shells that people gather from a beach are empty. The animals that made the shells died and disappeared long ago.

Without an animal to anchor it, a shell can be easily washed ashore by the force of ocean waves moving from sea toward land. On some sandy beaches waves wash up long lines of shells. But they may not be there long. With each **tide**—the daily changes in the level of the ocean—shells come and go.

Shells stack up on Sanibel Island, Florida

HUNTING FOR SHELLS

The easiest place to find sea shells is on a sandy beach, especially after a storm.

Most shells on the beach are chipped or broken from tumbling in the sea. Serious collectors look for unbroken shells.

Often, the only way to find an unbroken shell is to find a living snail or bivalve. Collectors dig in sand and mud in their hunt for live shells. Some collectors dive for shells or gather them by dragging nets from boats.

Young shell hunter examines a living lightning whelk before releasing it

USING SEA SHELLS

The beauty of shells makes them popular for collecting and trading. Collectors use shells for jewelry, decorations and displays.

Shells that are both beautiful and rare are very valuable. Some shells have become rare because too many have been taken by collectors. Others have become rare because the shell animals have been used for food.

To help save living shells, some communities limit the number that people can collect. Collecting live shells is not permitted at all in other places.

Glossary

bivalve (BI valv) — clams and other mollusks with two matching, joined shell sections

foot (FOOT) — a fleshy organ that extends from a snail body and is used for crawling

habitat (HAB uh tat) — the kind of place in which an animal lives, such as a sandy sea bottom

mantle (MAN tull) — the soft, shell-making part of a mollusk's body

marine (muh REEN) — of or relating to the sea, salt water

mollusk (MAHL usk) — a group of soft, boneless animals usually protected by hard shells of their own making; for example, clams, oysters, snails

organism (OR gan izm) — a living thing

predator (PRED uh tor) — an animal that kills other animals for food

species (SPEE sheez) — within a group of closely related animals, such as conch snails, one certain kind or type (*queen* conch)

tide (TIDE) — the daily rise and fall in the level of the ocean

INDEX